Five-Minute
art IDEAS
print

Edited by
Nicola Wright

Designed and illustrated by
Chris Dymond

Contents

zigzag

Hints and Tips

Before you start making any of the fun ideas in this book, put on old clothes so that it won't matter if you get messy.

Keep some scrap paper handy for trying out your prints before you use your good paper.

Cover your work area with old newspapers before you start in case anything spills.

Always ask an adult to help when using sharp objects such as craft knives. You can buy round ended safety scissors from most craft shops or stationers.

There are lots of different types of glue that can be used to stick objects to a block or card so you can print with them. For the Sticky Prints on pages 10 and 11, you will need to mix up some paste glue with water.

There are many different types of paint that you can use to print with. Poster paint is one of the best.

It is a good idea to keep pieces of scrap paper, cloth and other bits and pieces you have collected in a box ready to use when you need them.

Remember to clean your brushes after using them and to tidy up afterwards!

3

Handy Prints

You need

Paint

Scissors

Glue

Wallpaper lining paper

Plate

1

Pour some paint on a plate. Place the palm of your hand in the paint and then press down on to lining paper.

2

Make lots of hand prints, in different colours.

3

When the paint is dry, cut around each palm shape.

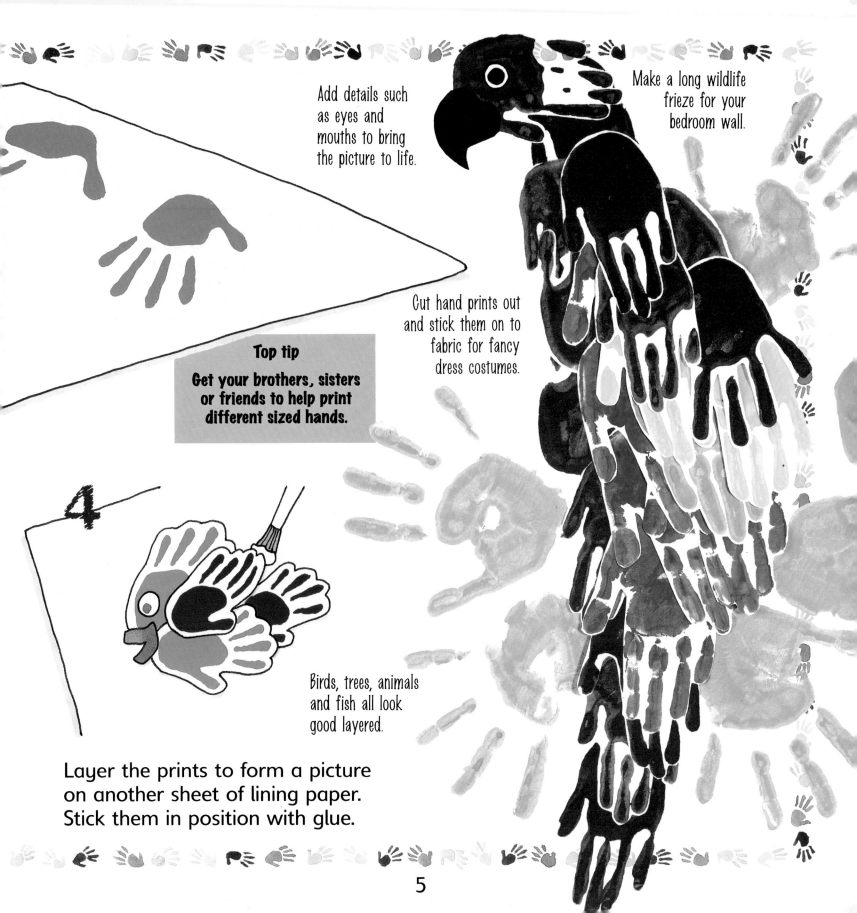

Add details such as eyes and mouths to bring the picture to life.

Make a long wildlife frieze for your bedroom wall.

Cut hand prints out and stick them on to fabric for fancy dress costumes.

Top tip

Get your brothers, sisters or friends to help print different sizes hands.

Birds, trees, animals and fish all look good layered.

Layer the prints to form a picture on another sheet of lining paper. Stick them in position with glue.

String Prints

You need

Parcel string (cotton)

Card

Glue

Paint

Brush

Ink roller

Coloured paper

1 Draw a simple picture on to thick card. Cover the card with glue and stick string where you have drawn. Wait for the glue to dry.

2 Brush paint evenly on to the string. Lay paper over the top and roll over the back of it with an ink roller. Peel back carefully.

Instead of an ink roller, you could use a rolling pin or milk bottle.

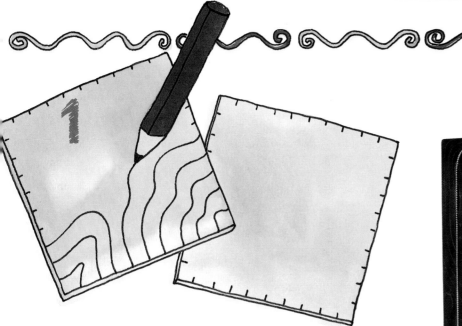

Cut two pieces of card 10cm x 10cm and make marks 1cm apart down the sides. Draw wavy lines to link the dots.

Use as wrapping paper and make a card and gift tag to match.

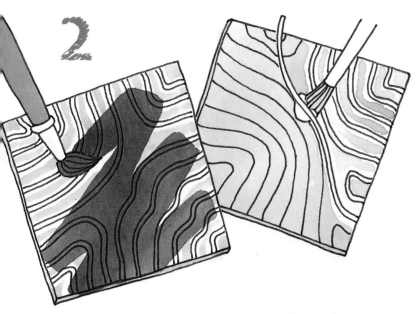

Glue string and cover with paint as before.

Roll over the back with a roller.

Press down in one corner of a sheet of paper. Line the other card up to the first and print again, then the first one again, until the whole sheet is covered.

Odds and Ends

You need

Everyday objects from around the house

Paint

Paper

Saucers

1

Find small objects around the house that are good shapes and have a flat surface. Ask an adult if the objects you have picked are alright to use.

2

Put some different coloured paint into saucers.

Dip your object into the paint and then press it down firmly on to a sheet of paper. Build up a pattern by using different shapes and colours.

Cork

Rubber

Bottle top

Peg

Fork

Pencil end

Top tip

If the objects you use are needed again, use a water based paint so that they can be washed.

3

Sticky Prints

You need

Smooth, wipeable surface

Paste glue

Powder paint

Newspaper

Paper

1

Put one colour paint one side of the glue, and another colour on the other side to get a multi-colour print.

Place a dollop of glue in the centre of a smooth, wipeable surface. Add a small spoonful of powder paint to the glue.

2
Mix the powder and glue together with your finger and spread the mixture over the surface.

3
Draw a pattern or shape in the mixture. Then place a sheet of paper over it. Then lay a piece of newspaper over the top.

Press the newspaper down hard, smoothing across the whole surface.

Remove the newspaper and then carefully peel the white paper off, starting at one corner. Leave to dry.

Top tip

Use a glue pattern as a background for a picture, for example, water. Stick a glue-drawn shape on top, for example, a fish.

If you draw a shape in the glue, you can cut it out and stick it on top of a pattern.

Veggie Prints

You need

Fruit and vegetables

Thick paper

Paint

Saucers

2

Put the paint into the saucers and dip your pieces of fruit and vegetable in them.

1

Ask an adult to cut up the fruit and vegetables for you. Try cutting different shapes into them.

Mushroom (without stalk)

Broccoli head

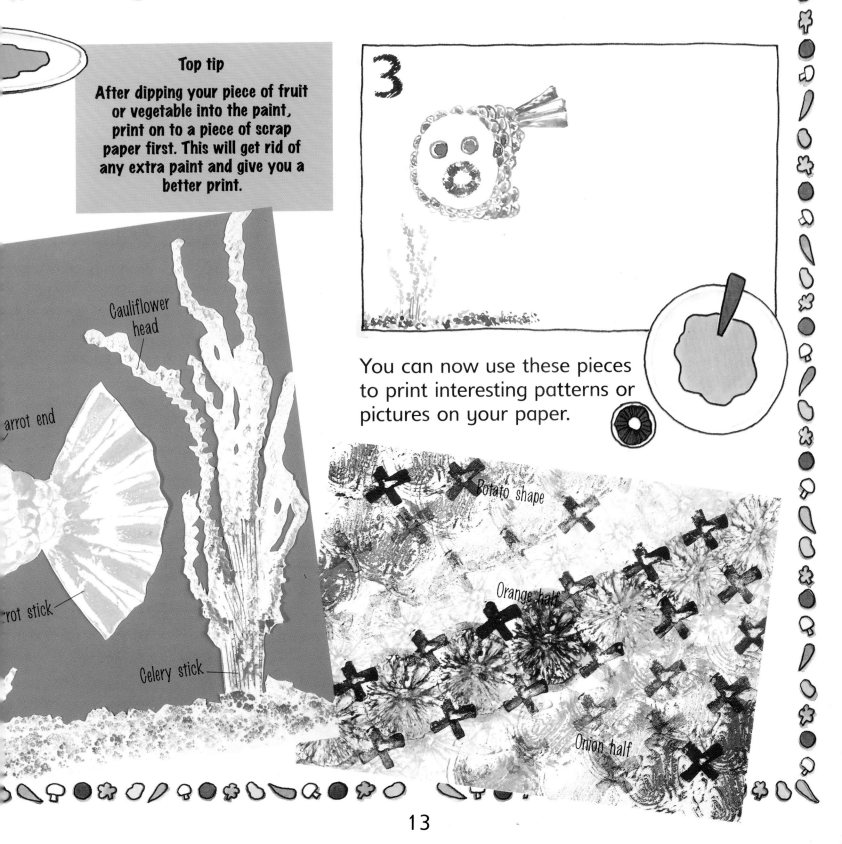

Top tip

After dipping your piece of fruit or vegetable into the paint, print on to a piece of scrap paper first. This will get rid of any extra paint and give you a better print.

3

You can now use these pieces to print interesting patterns or pictures on your paper.

Cauliflower head

arrot end

rot stick

Celery stick

Potato shape

Orange half

Onion half

Rag Printing

You need

Rags

Saucer

Scissors

Paint

Paper

Rubber band

Using the open or closed end of the rag to print with will give different effects.

1 Twist and scrunch up a rag. Hold the shape together with a rubber band wrapped round tightly.

2 Dip the end of the rag into some paint in a saucer and print on to a sheet of paper.

3

Use other rags to print different colours.

4

When the paint is dry, turn the paper over and draw shapes. Cut them out and stick down to make pictures.

Block Printing

You need

Paper

Paint

Glue

Block of wood

String, feathers, bottletops etc.

Plate

White paint on coloured paper looks good.

1 Look around the house for interesting objects to print from. Glue them on to a block in a pattern. Wait for the glue to dry.

String

You could use a block of polystyrene instead of wood.

Milk bottle top

2 Pour some paint on to a plate. Press the patterned side of the block into the paint and then on to paper.

Feather

Marbling

You need

Baking tray

Oil based paint

Water

White spirit

Vinegar

Brush

Paper

1 Fill a baking tray almost to the rim with water. Add a few drops of vinegar to the water.

2 Now mix your paint with some white spirit to make it thin and drop small amounts of different coloured paints into the water.

18

3

Lay a sheet of paper on the water. Wait for a couple of seconds and then lift it off.

4 Leave the paper to dry and you will see your marbled effect.

You could use the paper to wrap presents, or cut shapes out of it and stick on to card to make pictures.

Top tip

If you put wallpaper paste into the water as well as vinegar, your pattern will set even better.

Rolling Pin

You need

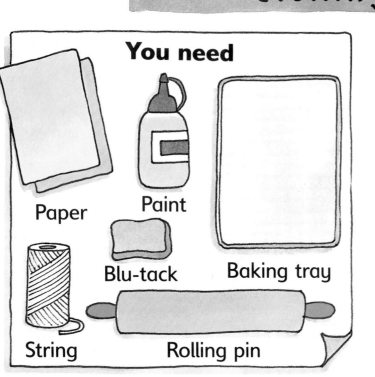

Paper

Paint

Blu-tack

Baking tray

String

Rolling pin

1 Tie a piece of string at one end of a rolling pin. Wind the string tightly around the pin until you reach the other end and tie it.

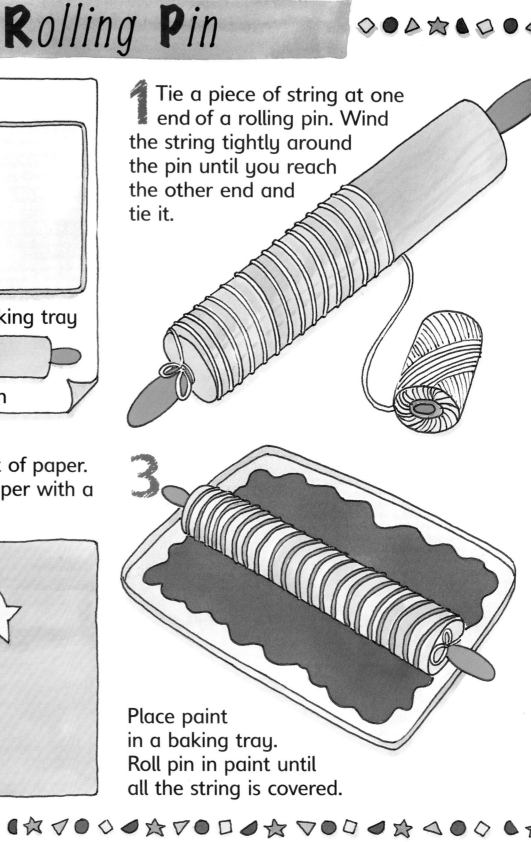

2 Tear or cut shapes out of paper. Stick the shapes on paper with a little Blu-tack.

3

Place paint in a baking tray. Roll pin in paint until all the string is covered.

You can do lots of different things using the rolling pin. Paint a tiger, leaving out the stripes. Then go over it with the rolling pin and it will look like a tiger in long grass.

4

Roll over the shapes again in a different direction to create a checked pattern.

Roll over the paper and shapes. When paint is dry, peel off the shapes.

Use the shapes to make pictures.

Pizza Prints

You need

Sheet of polystyrene e.g. a pizza base

Brush

Paper

Pencil

Paint

Saucer

Draw deeper lines for your main outline.

1

Draw a shape lightly on to a sheet of polystyrene. Once you are happy with it, go over the lines again pressing quite heavily so that an indented line is made.

Draw shallower lines for details such as fur and faces.

2

Quickly paint over the whole surface and then press facedown on to a sheet of paper.

Top tip
Wipe your polystyrene with a damp cloth if you want to print with another colour.

Don't use too much paint and try not to get it in the lines.

More Ideas

Use your thumbs and fingers to create different pictures.

You need an inkpad.

Complete your picture by drawing details in with a pen.

Produced by Zigzag Publishing Ltd, The Barn, Randolph's Farm, Brighton Road, Hurstpierpoint, West Sussex BN6 9EL, England.

Series concept: Tony Potter
Series editor: Paul Harrison
Cover designer: Nicky Chapman
Ideas by Sue Cleary, Pat Thornton, Sue Partington, Georgina Fenn, Lisa Nutt
Photographs by Zul Mukhida

Colour reproduction by Sussex Repro, England
Printed in Hong Kong

ISBN 1-85993-036-0 PB
ISBN 1-85993-070-0 HB